From Seashells to Smart Cards

Money and Currency

ERNESTINE GIESECKE

Heinemann Library
Chicago, Illinois

Designed by Herman Adler Design
Printed and bound in the United States by Lake Book
Manufacturing, Inc.

07 06 05 04 03
10 9 8 7 6 5 4 3 2 1

Library of Congress Cataloging-in-Publication Data
Giesecke, Ernestine, 1945-
  From seashells to smart cards : money & currency /
Ernestine Giesecke.
    v. cm. — (Everyday economics)
Includes bibliographical references and index.
Contents: What is money? — Earning money — Money long
ago — Early coins — Early paper money — Early American
money — How are coins made? — What coins do we use? —
How is paper money made? — What paper money do we
use? — What's on our money — Commemorative coins —
Fake money — Gold — Money around the world —
Exchanging money — Euro money — Other "money" —
Keeping money safe — Coin collecting & coin rubbing.
  ISBN 1-58810-491-5 (HC), 1-58810-954-2 (Pbk.)
1. Money—Juvenile literature. 2. Paper money—Juvenile
literature. 3. Coins—Juvenile literature. [1. Money. 2. Paper
money. 3. Coins.] I. Title.
HG221.5 .G54 2002
332.4—dc21

2002000803

Acknowledgments
The author and publisher are grateful to the following for
permission to reproduce copyright material:
Cover photographs by (L) W. Cody/Corbis and (R) Layne
Kennedy/Corbis
pp. 2, 20, 21 Bureau of Engraving and Printing; p. 4T Jeff
Greenberg/PhotoEdit, Inc.; pp. 4R, 5T, 6, 43B David Young-
Wolff/PhotoEdit, Inc.; pp. 4B, 36 Michael
Newman/PhotoEdit, Inc.; pp. 5B, 16, 17, 23, 26T U.S.
Mint; p. 7 Amy Etra/PhotoEdit, Inc.; pp. 9, 10, 11, 13B, 14,
15T, 15B, 18, 19, 24, 25, 26B, 27, 28, 29, 32, 33B, 34, 35,
38, 42, 44 2001 American Numismatic Society; p. 12 The
Art Archive; p. 13T Svenska Numismatiska Föreningen; p.
15C Courtesy of the Museum of the American Numismatic
Association; p. 30 FRBNY Archives; p. 31 Bettmann/Corbis;
p. 33T Jeffry W. Myers/Corbis; p. 37 AFP Photo/Joel
Nito/Corbis; p. 39 Tony Freeman/PhotoEdit, Inc.; p. 40
Michael Brosilow/Heinemann Library; p. 41 PhotoDisc; p.
43T Spencer Grant/PhotoEdit, Inc.; p. 45T Myrleen F.
Cate/PhotoEdit, Inc.; p. 45B Robert Lifson/Heinemann
Library

Every effort has been made to contact copyright holders of
any material reproduced in this book. Any omissions will be
rectified in subsequent printings if notice is given to the
publisher.

J
332.4
Gie
Mavin

Note to the Reader: Some words are shown in
bold, **like this.** You can find out what they mean
by looking in the glossary.

Contents

What Is Money?

Money is a method of exchange—it can be given in exchange for things people want and need. Money gives people a way to purchase **goods**, such as books, shoes, and compact discs; and **services**, such as car repair, firefighting, and pet grooming. Businesses and individuals accept money as payment for their goods and services. Governments accept money for payment of taxes and **debts**.

Money is important for other purposes besides exchange. It sets the standard of how much things are worth. You can use money to compare

Money lets you buy goods, compare the value of items, and save for something you want to buy at a later time.

the value of things. For example, a pair of jeans with a price of $40 is worth more than a pair of jeans that cost $20. A car valued at $12,000 is worth less than a car valued at $24,000. Dollars help specify price in the same way that hours specify the time.

Money has a third purpose, too. Money can be stored, or saved, to be used in the future. You can save the five dollars your aunt gave you on your ninth birthday

The money you pay for taxes helps pay for public services. The work others do for you can be very important.

until you are twelve years old, or even twenty. It will still be worth five dollars, no matter when you finally use it. People also use gold, jewelry, and other items as stores of wealth.

Printing paper money and making coins are the responsibilities of national governments. Any coins, paper money, or other **currency issued** by a government as official money is known as legal tender.

Know It

Legal tender

The verb *tender* can mean "to offer something in payment." Thus, money used to pay a debt is called legal tender. Each U.S. bill must have a statement identifying it as legal tender.

THIS NOTE IS LEGAL TENDER FOR ALL DEBTS, PUBLIC AND PRIVATE

Treasurer of the United States.

Earning Money

People earn money by working. The money people get for their work is called **income.** Some people earn income in the form of **wages.** Wages are income based on the number of hours worked or the number of items produced. For example, a checker at a grocery store may earn $6.50 for each hour he or she works. A factory worker may earn $0.40 for each belt or purse he or she produces.

Other people earn a **salary.** A salary is an income that remains the same for a fixed period of time, such as a year. For example, a secretary working in an office may earn a salary of $25,000 a year.

People use their income to buy the **goods** and **services** they need to survive. Their income pays for food, clothing, and shelter (or housing). Income also pays for services such as health care and police protection.

Know It

Some kinds of income, such as gifts, grants, and unemployment **benefits** are called **unearned income.** No goods or services are involved in unearned income.

At a video store, customers make choices about what game to buy. They have already made a choice to spend money.

Spending money is a way of making choices. You may buy a video game rather than save your money. Or, you may buy a software program to help you learn math. Either way, you have made a choice about what to do with your money.

Once you spend the money for the video game or the software program, you no longer have it to use for anything else. However, the money did not disappear. Some of it goes to the store, to pay the wages of the store clerk and to pay for the items you purchased. The video game company and the software company use the money from your purchases to pay the people who made the video game and developed the software. The companies will also buy supplies to make more video games and software. The money you spend in one place can end up in many different faraway places, in the hands of many different people.

The money you spend for a DVD player will eventually reach the worker who made the DVD player.

"Gone" but not lost

Did you think that once you spend your money it's "gone"? Well, it's not. It's simply moved along to the seller. The seller, in turn, will spend it in another market. This is how money moves through the **economy.** The system works only as long as people and companies can act as both buyers and sellers.

Money Long Ago

In early societies, a baker might trade five loaves of bread for two fish. A hunter might exchange half a roast deer for three new baskets. Today, you might trade your cheese sandwich for a chocolate milk. These are examples of **bartering**, directly exchanging one item for another.

Bartering can be difficult. Suppose the baker does not like fish. What if the basket maker wants fish, not deer? What if your friend wants orange juice, not a cheese sandwich? What can you trade for the chocolate milk? Problems like these can be solved using money.

Money is a **commodity**—an item that people agree to accept in trade. People in different places and times use different items as money. Often, the commodity they use is chosen because it is convenient. For example, each piece of the commodity should have a consistent, or standard, value. That way it does not have to be measured or weighed each time it is used. The item used as money should also be easy to divide into units that can be used to make small purchases. Also, money should be easy to carry from one place to another. This last feature of money has helped to increase trade around the world.

Know It

Salty times

In ancient Roman times, salt was one commodity that was used as money. Roman soldiers were sometimes paid in salt— or *salarium* in Latin. The word **salary** comes from this root.

10,000 B.C.E.	9000–6000 B.C.E.	2500 B.C.E.	1200 B.C.E.
People begin to barter, exchanging one item for another.	Cattle, sheep, camels, and wheat are used as money.	Ancient Mesopotamian records describe using weighed amounts of silver for payments.	Cowrie shells are used as money in India, Thailand, and Africa. This is probably the most widely accepted and longest used **currency** in history.

Use it or spend it!

In the past, people used salt; stones; tobacco; and strings of beads, cocoa beans, or seashells for money. Copper rings as well as pieces of gold and silver made convenient and **durable** money.

500 B.C.E.
The first coins, developed out of lumps of electrum, a natural mixture of gold and silver, appear in Lydia (now Turkey).

C. 1000 C.E.
The first paper money appeared in China.

1535 C.E.
The earliest known wampum, strings of beads made from clam shells, is used in North America.

1601 C.E.
The first western paper currency appears in Sweden.

Early Coins

Over time, lumps of metals such as gold or silver became acceptable for payment, so governments began to **issue** coins. Coins can be produced by stamping a design into a blank piece of metal. The process of making a coin is called minting.

King Croesus of Lydia (now western Turkey) issued the first gold coins in about 550 B.C.E. The Lydian coins were stamped with the king's **emblem,** the facing heads of a lion and a bull. About 500 years later, Emperor Augustus of Rome established a gold **currency,** the aureus. The aureus became the standard for trade payments throughout the Roman Empire and helped the Roman **economy** grow.

This Lydian coin carries the image of a lion. The stamped design was meant to show that the King of Lydia guaranteed the coin's value.

Know It

Biblical penny
A coin frequently referred to in the Bible is the denarius. It was a silver coin used by the ancient Romans.

Heads or tails

The "heads" side of the coin generally displays a portrait of a president, king, queen, or other national leader. On some coins, the "heads" side may show an animal important to a country's history, such as a horse, boar, lion, kangaroo, swan, or elephant. The opposite side of the coin is sometimes called the "tails" side.

The design of coins can vary widely. Because governments can control the size, shape, weight, material, and color of coins, they can set a specific value for each coin.

Early coins had their weights stamped on them so that they did not need to be weighed for each **transaction.** Sometimes the stamp also indicated the quality of the metal used to make the coin. Together, the weight and quality determined the coin's value—a value that was guaranteed.

Coins made of precious metals are an example of **commodity** money. Each coin has a specific value, based on what kind of metal it contains and how much that metal is worth. A coin with the same design, but made from a different metal, would have a different value based on the kind of metal used.

Early Paper Money

The first paper money was printed in tenth-century China, after the invention of block printing. Paper money had one main advantage over money stamped from gold, silver, or copper—paper was easier to carry from one location to another.

Know It

Flying money

Some Chinese paper money was equal in value to 1,000 coins. That many coins could weigh as much as 8 pounds (3.5 kilograms). Paper money was much easier to carry around. An early name for ancient Chinese paper money was "flying money" because it tended to blow away in a breeze.

In about 1300 C.E. the Chinese produced "paper" money using thin notebook-sized sheets of mulberry bark. The sheets carried the emperor's **seal** as well as the signatures of the country's treasurers.

The earliest European paper money was **issued** by Sweden in 1601. At the time, silver coins were in short supply. The Bank of Stockholm issued **bank notes** that were worth 100 dalers. A daler was a Swedish silver coin.

The paper money most countries issue is representative money. Unlike **commodity** money, representative money is not worth anything by itself. For example, the paper a dollar is made from has little value on its own, but it can be worth something if it is exchanged for a specific commodity, such as gold or silver. Bus and game tokens are also examples of representative money. They can be exchanged for a specific **service**, but that is their only value.

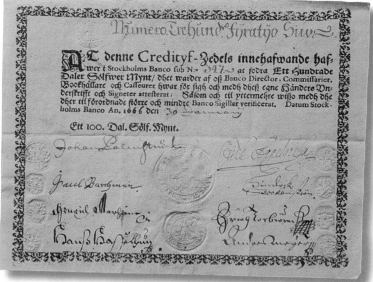

This is an example of the earliest European paper money. The Swedish note had to be signed by bankers and stamped with their official seals before it could be used.

Silver certificates

This United States silver certificate could be **redeemed** for a specific amount of silver. In 1967, Congress authorized the U.S. Treasury to stop redeeming silver certificates.

Early American Money

Money of any kind was scarce in the American colonies. The British government put strict limits on bringing British coins to the colonies. In addition, colonists were not allowed to mint any coins.

As a result, the colonists used any coins they could get. Spanish dollars were among those used most often. These coins came to the colonies through trade with the West Indies. The colonists gave these Spanish coins values in terms of English pounds, shillings, and pence. French and Dutch coins also **circulated** in the colonies.

Even so, the colonists were often short of cash. In some instances, they **bartered** for certain **goods** or **services**. In other instances, colonists kept book

Know It

Pieces of eight

Large silver Spanish dollars called "pieces of eight" were among the most common coins in the colonies. To make change, a person could chop the coin into eight pie-shaped pieces called bits. Two bits were worth a quarter of a dollar, four bits a half dollar, and so on. Some people still use the expression "two bits" to mean a quarter of a dollar, or 25 cents.

accounts. This system allowed people to pay for goods and services over time with their own goods and services. At times, colonial governments accepted **commodity** payments, such as beef, pork, corn, and rice.

In 1788, the United States Constitution gave Congress the power to coin money and control its value throughout the colonies. In 1792, Congress set up the first national money system in the United States. They named the dollar as the basic unit of money. At the same time, Congress established a national mint in Philadelphia, Pennsylvania. The mint produced ten-dollar gold coins called eagles, as well as silver dollars and other coins.

The U.S. Mint **issued** the eagle, a ten-dollar gold piece, from 1795 to 1805 and from 1838 to 1933.

Wampum

Native Americans made beaded necklaces or belts out of shells. These were known as wampum. Wampum came to be used as money in trade between the Native Americans and the colonists. Sometimes, colonists also traded wampum belts among themselves.

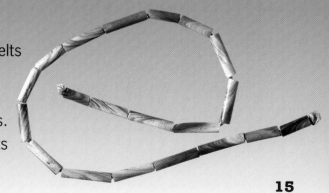

How Are Coins Made?

In the United States, the responsibility for making coins belongs to the United States Mint. The production of a new coin begins after government officials select a design.

An artist, called an **engraver,** makes a large clay model of the coin. Then the engraver makes a mold of the clay model and uses that mold to produce a plaster cast. The plaster cast is used to make the **die** that will stamp the pictures onto the coins. The actual process of making coins requires several more steps.

After the coins are minted and inspected, they are counted and dropped into large bags. The bags are closed, sealed, and stored. When a new supply of coins is needed, trucks take the new coins to the **Federal Reserve Banks.** A Federal Reserve Bank distributes the coins to your local bank.

Know It

The U.S. Mint has $3.7 billion in annual **revenues** and 2,800 employees. It is the world's largest manufacturer of coins, medals, and coin-based consumer products.

The same 1792 law that established the mint made coin **defacement, counterfeiting,** and theft by mint employees punishable by death.

How coins are made

Step 1: The mint buys strips of metal to use in making the coins. Each strip moves through a machine called a press. The machine punches out round disks, called blanks, from the metal strip.

Step 2: The coin-shaped blanks move through a very hot furnace to soften them. Then they are put through a washer and dryer. The blanks are inspected, and any imperfect blanks are recycled.

Step 3: Each blank moves through a mill that produces a raised rim around its edge.

Step 4: The blanks go to the coining press next. Here, each side of the blank is stamped with the designs and writing that are specific to the coin.

Step 5: Finally, inspectors check each batch of newly minted coins.

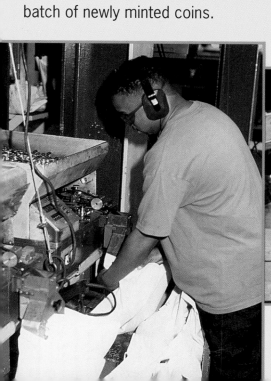

What Coins Do We Use?

There are six types of coins currently used in the United States. Each coin has a set value and a distinctive front and back. In the U.S., the size of a coin is not an indicator of how much it is worth. Most of today's coins have a copper center, covered with layers of an **alloy** made of copper and nickel. The copper-nickel mixture used to make coins is different for each coin value. Nickel has magnetic properties, so coins made with nickel can be sorted by **electromagnetic** devices.

Long lasting

A United States coin minted today will last about 30 years.

In addition to having different compositions, each kind of coin has a size and weight different from other coins.

Denomination:	Cent	Nickel	Dime
Face	Abraham Lincoln	Thomas Jefferson	Franklin D. Roosevelt
Back	Lincoln Memorial	Monticello	Torch, Olive Branch, Oak Branch
Edge	Plain	Plain	Ridged
Value	100 to a dollar	20 to a dollar	10 to a dollar

Also, some coins have ridges, called reeding, around their edges. These features help people with limited vision—as well as some mechanical coin sorters—to tell one coin from another more easily.

The Golden Dollar is the newest coin to be **issued.** Congress realized that a dollar coin was needed and passed the United States Dollar Coin Act in 1997. The dollar coins make vending machine **transactions** faster and more convenient. Even though it is called the Golden Dollar, it is not made of gold. The alloy it is composed of has a golden color.

Denomination:	Quarter	Half Dollar	Golden Dollar
Face	George Washington	John F. Kennedy	Sacagawea
Back	Eagle	Presidential Coat of Arms	Eagle in Flight
Edge	Ridged	Ridged	Plain
Value	4 to a dollar	2 to a dollar	1 to a dollar

How Is Paper Money Made?

Paper money is not made at the U.S. Mint, like coins. Instead, it is printed at the U.S. Bureau of Engraving and Printing in Washington, D.C.

Step 1: The production of a new **bank note** begins when an artist sketches the design for it. The Secretary of the Treasury approves the final design.

Step 2: Engravers then cut the design into a steel plate. A press squeezes the engraved plate against a soft steel roller, making a raised design on the roller's surface.

Step 3: Then the roller is heat-treated to harden it. Another press transfers the design from the roller onto a printing plate. Each plate prints 32 bills on one side of a sheet. Separate plates print the back sides of the bills.

Know It

Tower of cash

A stack of **currency** one mile high would contain over fourteen million bills.

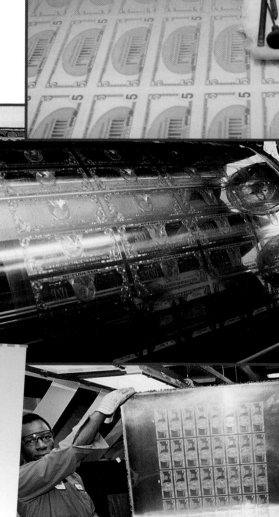

U.S. bills measure 2.61 inches (6.6 centimeters) wide by 6.14 inches (15.6 centimeters) long. Each bill is .0043 inches (.0109 centimeters) thick. If all the bills ever printed were laid end to end, they would stretch around the equator approximately 24 times.

Cloth money?

The paper in paper money is not really paper! U.S. paper money is printed on thin sheets made of 25 percent linen and 75 percent cotton. This makes the money **durable** and gives it a special "feel."

Step 4: Each bill passes through two presses. The design is printed first; then the **seals** and **serial numbers** are added.

Step 5: The large sheets are cut into stacks of bills.

Step 6: The bills are inspected, and imperfect bills are replaced with new ones called star notes. The star note has the same serial number as the bill it replaces, except that the last digit is replaced with a star.

Step 7: The bills are shipped to **Federal Reserve Banks,** and then distributed from there to commercial banks.

The Department of the Treasury will **redeem** a bill if:
- more than half of an identifiable bill is present; or
- one-half or less of an identifiable bill is present, and the Treasury is convinced that the missing portions have been totally destroyed.

Common causes of damage include fire, water, chemicals, explosives, animals such as rats or dogs, and deterioration by burying.

What Paper Money Do We Use?

Today's money, both coins and paper money, is fiat money. Fiat money has little value of its own and cannot be **redeemed** for a **commodity** such as gold or silver. People use fiat money to pay for **goods** and **services** because they are confident that it will be accepted as payment.

The **Federal Reserve Bank** is responsible for making sure that the value of U.S. **currency** does not change greatly. To do this, the government controls the amount of money in **circulation.** If prices stay the same, people can be confident that the dollar they use today to buy goods and services will buy a similar amount in the future.

The Federal Reserve circulates seven types of paper currency in the U.S. Unlike coins, all U.S. bills are the same color, size, and shape. However, bills of different values have different portraits and designs.

	Portrait on front	Design on back
$1	 George Washington	 "One" between face and back of the Great **Seal** of U.S.
$2	 Thomas Jefferson	Monticello (up to year 1976) or "Signing of the Declaration of Independence" (after year 1976)

	Portrait on front	**Design on back**
$5	 Abraham Lincoln	 Lincoln Memorial
$10	 Alexander Hamilton	 U.S. Treasury
$20	 Andrew Jackson	 The White House
$50	 Ulysses S. Grant	 U.S. Capitol
$100	 Benjamin Franklin	 Independence Hall

What's on Our Money

Motto: The national **motto,** "In God We Trust," must appear on all coins and paper **currency.**

Inscription: Words stamped on a coin form an inscription. U.S. coins must carry the word "Liberty."

Rim: The rim, a raised edge on both sides of a coin, protects the coin's design from wear.

Date: By law, coins must show the year they were made.

Edge: The edge is sometimes considered the third side of a coin. It is the outer border of a coin and may be plain or ridged.

Mint Mark: A small letter identifies where a coin was minted. Coins minted in Denver are marked with a *D*, while a *P* appears on coins minted in Philadelphia (except the penny). Coins minted in San Francisco are marked with an *S*, and coins minted in West Point are marked with a *W*.

Motto: All U.S. coins must carry the Latin motto *E Pluribus Unum,* meaning "out of many, one." This motto refers to the creation of the United States from the original thirteen colonies.

Legend: A legend is the description or title on a coin. It tells the coin's value.

Initials: Each **circulating** coin features the initials of its designer.

1 Federal Reserve Indicators:

Each bill bears the **seal** of the **Federal Reserve Banks.** The letter and number of the Federal Reserve Bank that **issued** the bill appear above the left **serial number.**

2 Legal Statement:

The phrase "This note is legal tender for all **debts,** public and private," appears on every bill. It means that the bill can be used to repay any and all debts.

3 Plate Position Letters and Numbers:

These indicate the position of the note on the 32-subject printing plate. The letter appears at the upper left and the lower right of each bill.

4 Plate Serial Number:

The small number after the lower right plate position letter is the serial number of the printing plate used to print the note.

5 Treasury Seal:

The seal of the U.S. Department of the Treasury appears on all bills.

6 Serial Number:

The serial number appears twice on each bill. It includes two beginning letters, eight digits, and an ending letter. If a star is used instead of an ending letter, the bill is a replacement note. Replacement notes take the place of bills with errors or of those removed for tests.

7 Series Date:

The date indicates the year the bill was designed. If only minor changes are made, a letter follows the date—for example, 1996A or 1996B.

8 Signatures:

All U.S. currency is printed with the signatures of the Secretary of the Treasury and the Treasurer of the United States. Over time, different people have worked in these jobs, so you might see different signatures from bill to bill.

Commemorative Coins

Sometimes, Congress approves the **issue** of a coin to honor a certain place, event, or person. These special coins, called **commemorative** coins, are offered for sale to the public. Some commemorative coins are made of gold or silver. People may buy the coins in order to collect them. Others buy them as an investment, hoping their value will increase over time.

Commemorative coins can help raise funds for specific causes. For example, Congress recently approved plans to build a Capitol Visitor Center to welcome visitors and provide information about how Congress works. Congress also arranged for the issue of some commemorative coins to help raise funds for the center. Part of the price of each coin will go to help build, maintain, and preserve the Capitol Visitor Center.

A five-dollar gold coin, a silver dollar, and a silver-clad half-dollar coin commemorates the first meeting of Congress at the Capitol building in Washington, D.C.

Know It

Booker T. Washington

The first coin to feature an African American was the Booker T. Washington memorial half dollar, minted in 1950.

Females on coins

Susan B. Anthony and Sacagawea have appeared on circulating dollar coins. Queen Isabella of Spain, Eunice Kennedy Shriver, Virginia Dare (with her mother, Eleanor Dare), and Dolley Madison have also appeared on commemorative coins.

Among the recently-approved **circulating** commemorative coins are 50 new state quarters. From 1999 to 2008, a new quarter celebrating one of the 50 states will be issued about every ten weeks, in the same order that the states joined the Union. Each quarter's **reverse,** or back, will bear a design chosen by that state to honor its **unique** history, traditions, and symbols. Like all commemorative coins legislated by Congress and issued by the U.S. Mint, these special quarters are legal tender.

Oregon Trail

In 1926, the U.S. minted a coin commemorating the Oregon Trail. It is meant to show the spirit of the American Indian on the face of the coin.

Fake Money

Sometimes people print bills that are not real money. Making fake, or **counterfeit,** money is against the law. Large amounts of counterfeit money can cause great damage to our country's **economy.** It is impossible for the **Federal Reserve Bank** to control how much money is **circulating** if other people are circulating their own **currency** as well.

Everyone can take part in keeping our money supply safe by watching out for counterfeit money. If you think you have a counterfeit bill, look at it closely. Compare it to another bill of the same value and series.

Look for these features if you think a bill is counterfeit:

real $5 bill

- A genuine portrait looks lifelike. It stands out from the background. A counterfeit portrait is usually flat and its details tend to fade into the background.

- In a genuine bill, the fine lines in the border are clear and unbroken. On a counterfeit bill, the lines may be blurred and separated.

- The paper for genuine currency has tiny red and blue fibers within it. Counterfeit bills try to imitate these fibers by printing tiny red and blue lines on the paper.

- The quality of the paper is another thing to look for. A genuine bill is made of cloth-like paper, whereas a counterfeit bill is made with regular, copy paper.

- Lastly, the numeral on the lower right hand corner of the face of a genuine bill is printed with color-shifting inks. These inks change color when the bill is viewed from different angles. The ink appears green when viewed directly, but looks black when the bill is tilted.

security thread   watermark

A security thread is embedded in the paper of a real bill to the left of the portrait. There is also a watermark to the right of the portrait, depicting the same person— in this case, Andrew Jackson.

The redesigned currency **issued** in the past few years has several additional features to help protect against counterfeiting.

Look for the following features on the new $20 bills:

- The words "USA TWENTY" and a picture of a flag appear on a security thread that runs the width of the bill. The thread glows green under an ultraviolet light. This prevents counterfeiters from bleaching a $20 bill and using the paper to print a $50 or $100 bill.

- The words "USA 20" are repeated in the bottom left hand numeral "20" on the face of the bill in very small print.

- The large numeral "20" on the back of the $20 note is easy to read.

- Along the bottom of the portrait's oval are the words "The United States of America." The printing is so small that it is hard to copy.

Know It

If you had ten billion $1 bills and spent one dollar every second of every day, you would need more than 317 years to spend it all.

The new $5, $10, $20, $50, and $100 bills each have a security thread that glows a different color when exposed to ultraviolet light.
    $5 glows blue
    $10 glows orange
    $20 glows green
    $50 glows yellow
    $100 glows red

Gold

All countries accept gold in payment for international **debts.** Many counties keep a supply of gold so that they will be able to make any payments when needed. The world's governments hold about 42,000 short tons (38,000 metric tons or 38 million kilograms) of gold in their official stocks. Almost all this gold is in bricklike bars called **ingots.**

About 60 foreign central banks and international organizations store their gold at the **Federal Reserve Bank** of New York. This bank has the largest amount of gold kept at one location. Storage at the bank offers safety and convenience. Because of the location, countries can take part in quick, easy, and inexpensive gold **transactions.**

A standard gold bar is generally 7 inches x 3 5/8 inches x 1 3/4 inches (17.8 centimeters x 9.2 centimeters x 4.5 centimeters). A standard gold bar weighs about 400 ounces or 27.4 pounds (12.4 kilograms).

The United States stores its **bullion** at Fort Knox in Kentucky. At present, about 147.3 million ounces (10.1 million pounds) of gold are at Fort Knox. The stored gold usually has a value of around $42 per ounce.

Visitors are not allowed at Fort Knox—with no exceptions.

Know It

During times of war, some historic and priceless items have been placed at Fort Knox for safekeeping. The Declaration of Independence, the U.S. Constitution, the Articles of Confederation, Lincoln's Gettysburg Address, three volumes of the Gutenberg Bible, and Lincoln's second inaugural address have all been stored at Fort Knox.

Making Fort Knox

The construction of Fort Knox required 16,000 cubic feet (453 cubic meters) of granite, 4,200 cubic yards (12,233 cubic meters) of concrete, 750 tons (680 metric tons) of reinforcing steel, and 670 tons (608 metric tons) of structural steel.

Money Around the World

Each country has a basic unit of money. The money from different countries looks different and has different names. For example, in the United States, the basic unit is the U.S. dollar. Canada uses the Canadian dollar, Mexico the new peso, Great Britain the pound, and Japan the yen.

British and French settlers brought British and French coins and paper **currency** to Canada. However, the Native Americans continued to use traditional methods of payment—beads and blankets. Settlers often preferred to use furs, particularly beaver skins, and grain as money. As in the American colonies, pieces of eight, from the Spanish milled dollar, were widely available to use as money. Canada adopted the dollar in 1867. The first dollar bills **issued** by the Dominion of Canada appeared in 1870. Today, Canada uses the following coins: $2, $1, 25 cents, 10 cents, 5 cents and 1 cent. Canada issues paper currency as well.

Hard money

Canada introduced a new dollar coin in 1987. It was minted to replace the paper dollar, since those bills would no longer be issued after 1989. The front of the coin has an image of Queen Elizabeth II of the United Kingdom. The **reverse** of the coin features a loon. Because of the bird on this coin, it is often called a "loonie."

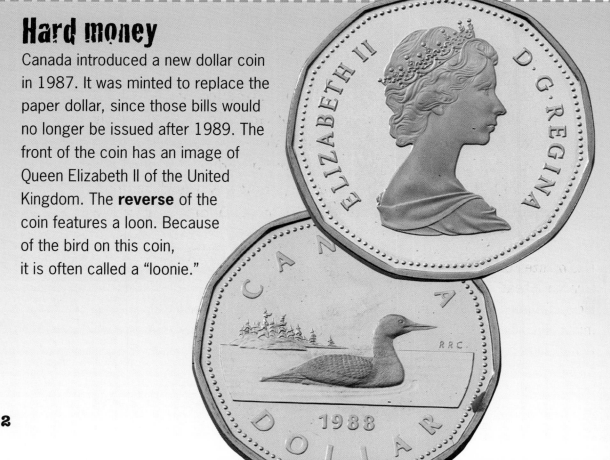

In January 1993, Mexico replaced its old peso with a new peso. One new peso equals 1,000 old pesos.

The new peso is the basic unit of currency in Mexico. The peso was the name of the old Spanish dollar. It was called the *peso de oro* when it was made of gold, and the *peso de plata* when made of silver. Mexican bills come in five **denominations:** 20, 50, 100, 200, and 500 pesos.

About 2,000 years ago, the ancient Romans and Celts introduced coins to Britain. Through trade, war, and colonization, Britain introduced its money to many parts of the world. Today, the regions of Great Britain—including England, Scotland, Northern Ireland, and Wales—use the pound sterling as the base for their currency. The pound sterling is divided into 100 pence, and its symbol is £. Because the pound was introduced in so many different places, it is one of the world's most important currencies.

Know It

Early coins contributed to worldwide trade. Not only did the coins eliminate the need for **bartering,** but people were willing to accept coins because their value was the same from one place to the next.

This bronze Roman coin has a head facing right on the front and a horse with a man's head on the reverse.

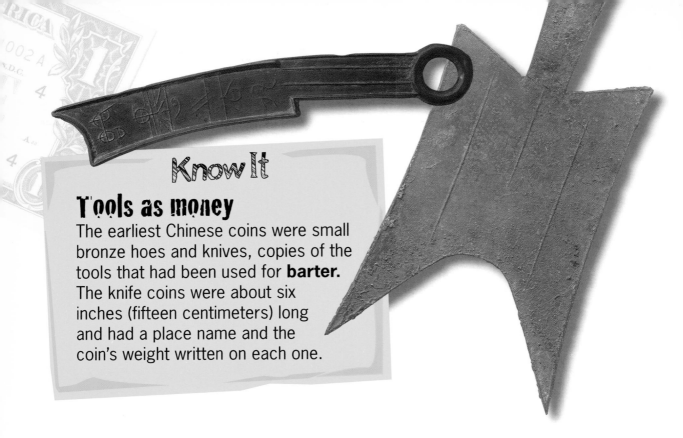

Know It

Tools as money

The earliest Chinese coins were small bronze hoes and knives, copies of the tools that had been used for **barter.** The knife coins were about six inches (fifteen centimeters) long and had a place name and the coin's weight written on each one.

The Chinese **issued** round coins, usually bronze, around the mid-third century B.C.E. In general, each round coin had a square hole, as well as four characters that meant "**circulating** treasure." Today, the **currency** of both the People's Republic of China and Taiwàn is based on a unit called the yuan.

The Chinese call their money "yuan," meaning "dollar." The 10 and 100 yuan notes carry political images.

Japan has issued both gold and silver coins since the 1600s. The gold coins were large flat pieces, rectangular in shape, with rounded corners. Today, Japanese money is based on the yen. Yen means "round coin." The symbol for yen is ¥.

The largest Japanese coin, the oban, was rectangular or oval. Obans were usually made as rewards and gifts.

Traditionally, people in Africa made payments using things such as cattle, cloth, and salt. Well into the 1900s, this was still an acceptable way to make a payment in Africa. Because much of Africa was divided into colonies ruled by the British, French, and Portuguese, there were many different kinds of currencies used in colonial Africa. Once the colonies gained independence, most issued their own currencies. Some of the names of these currencies are similar to the names of the money issued by the colonial powers. For example, Cameroon, Central African Republic, Niger, and Senegal all have a standard currency named the CFA franc, the unit of French currency common during colonial times.

The Japanese use coins of 1, 5, 10, 50, 100, and 500 yen. They use bills of 1,000, 2,000, 5,000, and 10,000 yen.

African money

Coins in the new South Africa show the national arms of South Africa as well as local plants and animals. The coins are inscribed in African languages such as Xhosa and Zulu.

Ghana was once a British colony. After Ghana gained its independence from Britain in 1957, it began issuing its own currency.

Exchanging Money

In today's world, countries buy **goods** and **services** from one another. For example, Americans buy French wine and Japanese cars. The French buy American blue jeans and Colombian coffee.

Most goods and services must be paid for in the **currency** of the country that sells them. Suppose a car dealer in the United States wishes to sell Japanese cars. The dealer must first buy the cars. He or she needs to pay for the cars with Japanese currency—the yen. In other words, the dealer must exchange, or trade, U.S. dollars to get Japanese yen. The dealer can use dollars to buy yen from a bank.

Know It

A country trying to sell goods and services to other countries may have trouble if its prices are too high. When this happens, it may choose to **devalue** its currency in relation to other currencies. Then its prices will not seem so high, but will be more in line with world markets.

A U.S. car dealer first needed yen to buy these Japanese cars before selling them for U.S. dollars.

FOREIGN EXCHANGE RATE BOARD

		Travellers Cheques We Buy At	Notes We Buy At	We Sell At
🇺🇸 USA	USD	5400	5423	
JAPAN	JPY	.4230	.4280	
…NY	DEM	22.78	23.28	
…LAND	CHF	29.60	30.10	
…KINGDOM	GBP	…99	7474	
…A	CAD	…29	3379	
…RALIA	AUD		27.11	
…NGAPORE	SGD		29.10	
…RANCE	FRF		6.93	

Banks and other financial firms buy and sell foreign currency. If they buy when the exchange rate is low, and they exchange the currency when the exchange rate is high, they can make money.

Being able to exchange the currency of one nation for the currency of another nation is important when buying and selling goods and services. If the currencies could not be exchanged, or converted, the U.S. car dealer would not be able to buy the Japanese cars. Fortunately, most of the world's currencies can be exchanged for one another.

The price the dealer must pay for the yen is determined by the currencies' exchange rate. An exchange rate is the price of one country's currency expressed in terms of another country's currency. For example, if the exchange rate were 1 U.S. dollar = 100 Japanese yen, the American car dealer would have to spend $15,000 to buy enough yen to pay for a Japanese car that cost 1,500,000 ¥.

Exchange rates change often, sometimes from one day to the next. This means that the next time the dealer wanted to buy Japanese products, he or she might need more dollars to buy the same number of yen.

European Money

For hundreds of years, countries such as Sweden, France, Germany, Italy, and Spain have had their own **currencies.** However, beginning in 1999, these European countries and seven others began to use a shared currency called the euro. Beginning in 2002, the countries stopped using their national currencies—only the euro is legal tender now. However, people are still able to exchange their previous national currencies at banks.

The countries who adopted the euro are members of the European Union, a group formed in 1993. Among the most important reasons the group formed was to make international trade, the buying and selling of **goods** and **services** between countries, easier among the member nations. Some of the nations thought that adopting a shared currency would be a good idea, because international trade would be easier if the countries all used the same kind of money. They hope that increased trade will make each country's **economy** stronger and bring the nations closer together politically.

There are eight euro coins: 1, 2, 5, 10, 20, and 50 cents, as well as 1 euro and 2 euros. The face of every euro coin of a particular value is the same. The **reverse** of each coin has a national symbol, each chosen by the particular participating country.

Top: All coins worth one euro have the same face. *Bottom:* The back, or reverse, of this particular euro coin shows a national symbol chosen by Italy.

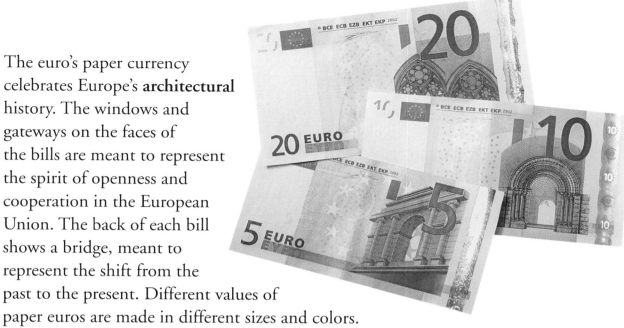

The euro's paper currency celebrates Europe's **architectural** history. The windows and gateways on the faces of the bills are meant to represent the spirit of openness and cooperation in the European Union. The back of each bill shows a bridge, meant to represent the shift from the past to the present. Different values of paper euros are made in different sizes and colors.

No matter what national symbol is on a coin or bill, it can be used anywhere within the twelve member states. For example, a German citizen could buy bread in Paris using a euro coin carrying the likeness of the king of Finland. Using the euro will make purchases within the twelve member nations easier, because there will be no need to exchange one currency for another.

Euro countries

Twelve nations of the European Union share the euro currency: Austria, Belgium, Finland, France, Germany, Greece, Ireland, Italy, Luxembourg, the Netherlands, Portugal, and Spain.

The symbol for the euro represents the first letter of the word "Europe." The parallel lines represent the stability of the euro.

Know It

Tall order

Issuing a common currency for twelve nations is an enormous task. The initial printing of paper euros, placed end to end, would stretch from Earth to the moon five times. The initial minting of coins, stacked one upon another, would be 1.4 million times the height of the Leaning Tower of Pisa.

Other "Money"

Ordinarily, when we think of "money," we think of the coins and bills in our pockets. However, today many people spend money without ever exchanging bills or coins.

A check is sometimes used to make an exchange of money. To pay by check, you must have a checking account at a bank with enough money in the account to cover, or match, the amount of the check. For example, to pay for a CD that costs $10, you might write a check to "CD Superstore" for $10. The check promises that your bank will pay CD Superstore $10 from your checking account. To collect the $10, CD Superstore must **deposit** your check in their bank account. Their bank will exchange it for $10 in coins and bills.

People often use checks instead of bills or coins to pay for something. A person or business accepting the check trusts that the check can be exchanged for **currency.**

NANCY DICKMANN   09-97

3333 W. DRUMMOND
CHICAGO, IL 60647

2-1/710 5010   539

Date _October 9, 2002_

Pay To
The Order Of _CD Superstore_ $ 10.00

Ten and _____ 00/100 Dollars

BANK ONE, NA
CHICAGO, ILLINOIS 60670
WWW.BANKONE.COM

For _Jon's Birthday_   _Nancy Dickmann_   MP

⑈07 10000 13⑆ 11 10000000090⑈ 00539

©CHECKS UNLIMITED™ • PLATINUM • www.ChecksUnlimited.com
TO REORDER: 1-800-204-2244

Sometimes people use a plastic card called a debit card, to make their purchases. Just as when using checks, to pay using a debit card, you must have a checking account with a bank and enough money in the account to cover the amount of your purchase. When the cashier at CD Superstore **swipes** your card through an electronic reader, the money for the purchase is **transferred** from your bank account to the bank account of CD Superstore.

Many of the small plastic cards people carry are credit cards. These cards are used to purchase **goods** and **services.** Credit cards give the user a choice on when to actually pay for their purchases. Some people pay the total amount of all their purchases when the monthly bill arrives. Others pay only a part of the total each month.

A new, popular way to pay for purchases—especially for telephone calls—is the "smart card." A smart card looks like a debit card. However, the smart card has a built-in computer chip that keeps track of several **transactions.** For example, you might purchase a phone card for $20. You use it to make a $2 long-distance call to your friend. When you swipe the card or dial a set of numbers, the $2 is automatically subtracted from the **balance** on the card. You still have $18 left to spend on phone calls.

Smart cards have a computer chip right on the card. The chip helps keep track of any purchases or deposits.

Keeping Money Safe

You can choose whether or not to spend the money you have. Often, people decide to save money for future purchases. Some save money so that they will have enough to live on when they are no longer working. Some save money to be prepared for unexpected expenses, like illness, accidents, or job loss.

In all of these cases, people want to keep their money in a safe place. Young people often keep some of their allowance and birthday money in a small container, or bank, at home. Over the years, there have been many types of banks, each designed to help people put some of their money away for safekeeping.

People who save large amounts of money often keep the money in a savings account at a bank. Banks usually offer many different kinds of savings accounts. When you **deposit** your money at a bank, the bank uses your money to make loans to other people. For example, the bank may use your money to give someone else a car loan or a loan to buy a

Pirates' bounty

One way pirates kept their money safe when they traveled was to bury it. They might draw a treasure map to help them find it again when they returned. One of the favorite treasure coins was a gold doubloon (duh BLOON). The doubloon is a Spanish and Spanish-American gold coin that was widely used in America until the 1800s. The doubloon was equal to sixteen silver dollars or eight gold *escudos*. It weighed slightly less than an ounce (about 27 grams).

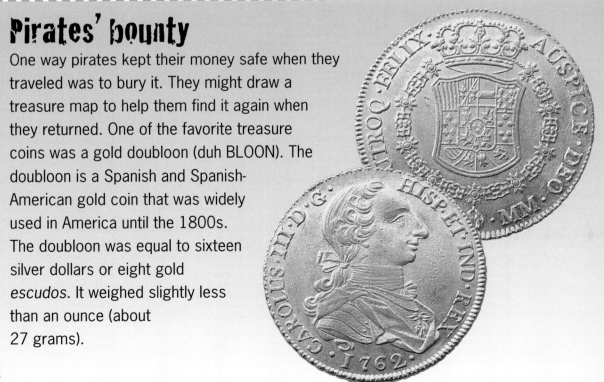

house. Most banks pay you **interest** on your accounts. Interest is an amount paid in return for the use of your money.

Once you decide to put your money in a bank, you should compare the offers different banks make. You should ask questions like these:

- Is there a **minimum** dollar amount needed to open a savings account?
- How much interest will the money earn?
- How often is the interest paid?
- Are there any **penalties** if you take your money out of the account?
- Does the bank have any other fees for services?

Compare the answers and deposit your money in the bank that best suits your needs.

Lazy money

Money in a savings account can work for you by earning interest. Money kept in a piggy bank does not work for you, as it will not earn interest.

Coin Collecting & Coin Rubbing

Coin collecting is one of the world's most popular hobbies. It began in the fifteenth and sixteenth centuries when people wanted to learn more about ancient Greek and Roman culture. Words and pictures on coins can give clues to the **economic**, political, and religious characteristics of a particular time. Coins can tell the story of famous people and events. For example, the portraits used on coins often provide reliable pictures of rulers. Other coin images help us to know what was important to the people and government of that time.

This $10 gold piece has a liberty cap on the front. However, the coin is called an eagle because of the bird shown on its back (see page 15).

Coin collectors often work towards a goal. They may try to collect a complete set of one nation's coins, or they may try to collect one coin from each country of the world. Other collectors are interested in coins of unusual shapes or sizes. Some collectors might even specialize in collecting coins with images of women, ships, animals, or plants.

You can start your own collection by deciding what subject or time period is of interest to you. Then, sort through the coins you get in change when you buy something. You can also go to a bank and purchase rolls of coins to examine. These coins will only be fairly recent U.S. minted coins.

Because Benjamin Franklin designed this copper coin, it is often called a Franklin cent. *Fugio* means "to fly." It was supposed to represent the **motto**, "Time flies."

Once you have collected some coins, you will need to take care of them. Protect the coins from dust, fingerprints, moisture, and scratches. Handle them as little as possible. If you need to pick up a coin, hold it by its edges. Some collectors put their coins in metal cabinets that have trays lined with soft cloth. Others use small paper envelopes designed to hold coins. Do not clean your coins—removing dirt may scratch the metal, making the coins less valuable.

Know It

Green money

You should never store your coins in plastic bags. The coins will turn green and their surfaces will be damaged.

Coin rubbing

One way to make a record of coins you like is to make rubbings of them. A rubbing allows you to record the face and **reverse** of a coin. To make a rubbing you will need:

- some lightweight paper such as tracing paper;
- a large metal ring or removable tape; and
- rubbing wax or a soft lead pencil.

1. Place your coin on a solid surface such as a table or desk.
2. Cover the coin with the tracing paper.
3. Hold the tracing paper in place with a large ring or with removable tape.
4. Gently rub the coin with rubbing wax or a soft lead pencil.
5. Be sure to record both the face and the reverse of your coin.

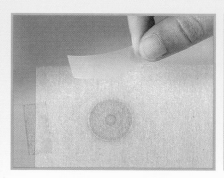

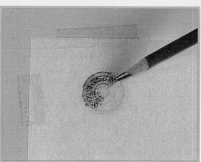

Glossary

alloy mixture of two or more metals

architectural related to buildings and other large structures

balance amount of money in an account

bank note piece of paper issued by a government-authorized bank and accepted as money

barter to trade by exchanging goods or services instead of money

benefit something that happens or is given for the good of a person; advantage

bullion gold or silver, especially in bars or ingots

circulate to spread widely among people or places

commemorative honoring the memory of someone or something

commodity item of trade

counterfeit made as a false copy of something, especially money, with the intent to defraud or cheat someone

currency means of exchange; money

debt something that is owed

deface to spoil or injure the surface of something

denomination one of a series of different values, as with money

deposit to put in, as money into a bank account

devalue to lower the value of something

die tool that shapes materials by stamping or punching

durable strong enough to withstand wear and tear and last for a long time

economy use or management of money

electromagnetic related to electricity or magnetism

emblem symbol

engraver artist who cuts or sculpts a design into a material

Federal Reserve Bank central banking system of the United States

good thing that can be bought and sold

income money earned through work

ingot mass of a metal, often shaped in the form of a brick

interest amount charged for the right to use or borrow money

issue to give out or distribute

minimum least possible amount

motto phrase expressing a guiding rule or idea

penalty punishment for breaking a rule; in banking, usually involves paying a fee

redeem to turn in one item in exchange for something else

revenue money collected by a government

reverse back of something, such as a coin

salary set amount of money paid for work over a certain period of time

seal design used to identify a person or a thing

serial number identification number that is
  part of a series of numbers

service work done for another or others

swipe to slide with a sweeping movement

transaction act of conducting business

transfer to move from one place
  to another

unearned income money received without
  doing anything for it

unique one of a kind

wage payment for work based on the
  number of hours worked or the rate of
  production

More Books to Read

Cribb, Joe. *Money.* New York: DK Publishing, 2000.

Macht, Norman. *Money and Banking.* Broomall, Penn.: Chelsea House,
  2001.

Simpson, Carolyn. *Choosing a Career in Banking and Finance.* New York:
  Rosen Publishing Group, 1999.

Index